I0837611

1. The Eccentric Girl

I met her online during my second year of college, back when everyone still thought dating apps were sketchy but secretly used them anyway. She was gorgeous in her photos — hazel eyes, a mischievous smile, and this effortless glow that made me double-check whether she was a model slumming it online. For three weeks, we texted constantly. She was funny, polite, and had this quirky way of phrasing things that made her sound both sophisticated and approachable. By the end of week three, I had convinced myself that this was the kind of woman people brag about meeting.

We decided on dinner at a trendy bistro downtown. I got there early — fifteen minutes early, to be exact — because I'm the type of guy who would  rather pace around the block than make someone wait. I sat at a corner table, rehearsing icebreakers in my head. I was ready for the sparkling conversation, the soft background jazz, maybe even that magical moment when you both reach for the bill and laugh.

Instead, I got forty minutes of sitting alone, pretending to study the menu while the waitress refilled my water and gave me increasingly sympathetic looks. My phone buzzed every so often with her texts: "Almost there!" then "Traffic's insane lol", then "Be there sooooon."

By the time she arrived, any excitement I'd had had curdled into irritation. And then she walked in, and — well.

She was shorter. Much shorter. And heavier. Not just the "people look different in person" kind of heavier, but the "those photos were taken at least five years and fifty pounds ago" kind of heavier. For a split

second, I considered whether this was even the same girl. But the eyes and smile gave her away.

"Sorry I'm late!" she chirped, sliding into the seat opposite mine like we were old friends meeting up, not two strangers awkwardly colliding.

I should have left right then. Any rational person would have. But no, not me. I was too polite, too stupid, too invested in the fantasy I'd built up.

We ordered. Or rather, she ordered. Four drinks. Two appetizers. The most expensive entrée on the menu. I hadn't even touched my glass of water yet.

"I'll have the lobster ravioli," she said with the enthusiasm of someone ordering at their favorite restaurant, not a girl meeting her date for the first time. She handed the menu back without looking at me, like the bill was already settled.

I sat there dumbly, trying to recalibrate.

Then came the compliments. And not normal compliments either.

"You're so tall," she said, eyes wide. "Like, so tall. You must hit your head on everything. And your hair — oh my god, it's practically golden. Do you dye it? You look like a Viking. A hot Viking. Our kids would be terrifyingly cute. Like, they'd probably break hearts in kindergarten."

I laughed weakly, wishing the tablecloth could swallow me whole.

Two drinks in, she leaned closer and dropped her voice. "You know what I can't stand? Mixed relationships. Like, ugh. Doesn't it just ruin the bloodline? People should stick to their kind, you know?"

My jaw clenched. I glanced at the bar, wondering if it would be rude to walk away mid-rant. By her fourth drink, her words slurred into a messy tirade about everything from her ex-boyfriend's "disgusting" habits to how every guy should pay on the first date because "it's only fair."

Finally, she excused herself to the restroom.

The moment she disappeared, I waved the waitress over. She was petite, sharp-eyed, with dark hair tied neatly back, and she wore the kind of smile that suggested she'd seen this scene play out before.

"Hey," I started, lowering my voice, "this date is... going downhill. Fast. She's ordered half the menu, and I'm not sticking around for dessert."

The waitress chuckled. "Don't worry, I've got you. Your meal's boxed up at the bar already."

That single sentence felt like salvation.

When my date's chair was still empty, I paid the bill in cash — slipping in a generous tip for the waitress's quick thinking — and left. The night air felt like freedom.

Back at my apartment, I unwrapped the takeout, only to find a folded napkin tucked beside the container. A phone number, scrawled in neat handwriting.

Underneath: "I get off at eleven. Want to try a better first date?"

For the first time that night, I grinned.

Later, the waitress — her name was Maya — told me what happened after I left. My date had returned to the table, found me gone, and pitched a tantrum loud  enough to draw the manager. When she admitted she hadn't brought any money, the situation escalated. Security finally got involved.

Eventually, the cops showed up. Her father had to drive an hour into town to bail her out of a dine-and-dash charge.

For weeks afterward, my phone buzzed with desperate texts: "Hey, can we talk?" "You didn't give me a chance." "Please call me."

I didn't.

Instead, I called Maya.

And our first date? Let's just say it didn't involve lobster ravioli, racial rants, or forty minutes of waiting.

2. Touchy Girl

It started in the most ridiculous, humiliating way imaginable.

I was in a crowded dive bar with friends, one of those places where the floor is sticky and the jukebox only plays rock from before I was born. After three beers, I excused myself to the restroom. It was dim, smelled like bleach failing to do its job, and had one urinal with a cracked tile wall behind it. Not exactly the setting for romance.

I was midstream, minding my business, when the door creaked open. I expected some drunk guy to stumble in. Instead, she walked in — this girl I'd been introduced to earlier at the bar, someone I barely knew. She smiled like she'd been waiting for this exact moment.

Before I could say a word, she stepped right up, reached out, and grabbed me.

I nearly jumped out of my skin. "What the hell are you doing?" I hissed.

"Relax," she said, tilting her head, eyes glittering with curiosity. "I just wanted to see how big you were."

I froze, half in shock, half in disbelief. She was holding me like it was the most natural thing in the world, like she'd just borrowed a pen without asking.

"You'll thank me later," she added with a sly grin. "We could have some fun right here. Nobody would notice."

She gestured toward the stall, a graffiti-smeared cubicle with a busted lock. The kind of place you don't even want to touch the door handle with your sleeve, let alone do anything intimate inside.

I pulled away and zipped up so fast I nearly caught myself in the zipper. "No way," I muttered. "This is insane."

Her smile flickered into a pout. "Wow. You're seriously saying no?"

"Yes. Absolutely."

She looked at me like I'd just insulted her entire existence. "Guess you're not into women then." And with that, she flounced out, leaving me standing there, furious and stunned.

I thought that would be the end of it. But it wasn't.

For weeks, she made me her project.

Every time we crossed paths at a party, a bar, even in the cafeteria, she'd sidle up to me with that same mischievous smile. If  she'd been drinking, it was worse.

Her hands were everywhere — grabbing at my waistband, sliding down my stomach, trying to force my hand up her skirt or under her blouse. It was constant, relentless.

The worst part? Nobody cared.

When I complained to my friends, they laughed. "Dude, what's the problem? She's hot. Just go with it."

Even other women brushed it off. "She's just flirty," they'd say. "Don't take it so seriously."

But it wasn't flirting. It was harassment. And I hated it.

I'd yank my hand back, step away, tell her to quit it. She'd giggle and call me "shy." If I snapped at her, she'd roll her eyes and tell everyone I was uptight, or — her favorite dig — that I must secretly not like women.

That one stuck. People started joking about it behind my back, then to my face. Every time I turned her down, she smirked like she'd won some invisible argument.

I can still remember one night vividly. We were at a house party, music blasting, bodies packed shoulder to shoulder. I was wedged into a corner, trying to carry a conversation with a buddy, when suddenly I felt her hand sliding down the back of my jeans. I shoved her away, harder than I meant to, and she staggered into the crowd. People saw, laughed, pointed.

"Easy, man," someone called out. "You'll hurt her feelings."

Hurt her feelings. As if my feelings weren't even part of the equation.

After that, I started avoiding certain parties, certain bars. If I knew she was going to be there, I stayed home. Friends called me dramatic. Some said I should be grateful for the attention. But I wasn't grateful — I was exhausted.

She turned every encounter into a joke at my expense, and everyone else played along.

And the thing that stung the most was realizing how quickly people dismissed it. If the roles had been reversed — if I'd cornered her in a bathroom, grabbed her without asking, badgered her for weeks — nobody would have laughed. It wouldn't have been a joke.

But because I was a guy, because she was a woman, it was entertainment. I still remember the sound of her laugh echoing through that disgusting bar bathroom, like she knew she could get away with anything.

And the truth is, she did.

3. Bar Girl

It was a Saturday night, the kind where the air already feels heavy with sweat and smoke before you even step into the bar. This was a place I went often, a familiar haunt with sticky tables, jukebox country songs no one really liked, and bartenders who knew my usual order before I opened my mouth.

I was three drinks in, comfortably tipsy, when she approached me.

She was big. Not just "a little curvy," not just "on the plus side" — she was clearly much larger than me, and I'm well over two hundred pounds. She walked up with a cigarette dangling from her fingers and asked for a light.

"Sure thing," I said, pulling mine from my pocket. I'm the type who can't say no to small favors, especially after a few beers.

The flame flickered between us, lighting her face for a brief second. She grinned, exhaled, and leaned against the wall beside me. Conversation followed — half idle chatter, half her slurring about how dead the bar scene had been lately. I nodded along, polite but not particularly interested.

When she finished her cigarette, she dropped it to the pavement and ground it out with her shoe. Then, without warning, she shifted her weight toward me.

"Let's do something else," she said, voice thick, breath hot.

Before I could react, her arm was around me. Heavy. Stronger than I expected. She pressed her body against mine, trying to force me into the wall.

"Whoa, hey — stop!" I said, shoving against her shoulder.

She tilted her face up, puckering her lips, aiming clumsily for a kiss.

"Get off me!" I shouted, louder this time. My palms braced against her, trying to create space, but she didn't budge. She had the weight advantage, and she was determined.

Panic surged in me. I wasn't flattered; I wasn't amused. I felt trapped. So I did the only thing I could think of: I pushed, hard.

She stumbled backward, arms flailing, and landed half-off the curb with a loud grunt. Her face twisted — not from pain, but from humiliation. She sat there, cheeks flushed, struggling to get her balance. For a moment I considered offering a hand, but the anger in her eyes froze me in place.

I turned and went back inside, dropped cash on the bar to cover my tab, and left.

I thought that was the end of it.

But the next weekend, when I walked through those same doors, the atmosphere felt different. A man I didn't recognize stepped in front of me before I could even reach the counter.

"You," he growled, jabbing a finger into my chest. "You're the guy who laid hands on her."

"What are you talking about?" I asked, trying to sidestep him.

He blocked me. "I should've taken you out back last week. Made you receive what you give."

The words hung heavy in the air. I felt eyes turning toward us, curious, suspicious.

"I didn't do anything," I said, heat rising in my voice. "She came at me. I told her no. She wouldn't stop."

"Don't lie," he spat. "She told us you pinned her on the sidewalk and left her there."

I stared at him, dumbfounded. "That's not what happened!"

But it didn't matter. The bartender, a guy I'd chatted with countless times before, leaned across the counter with a look that made my stomach drop.

"Best you leave," he said. His voice was calm, but the steel in it was unmistakable. "Don't come back. Next time, people are gonna call the cops."

I wanted to argue, to defend myself, to shout the truth until they believed me. But I could see it in their faces: the verdict had already been decided.

So I walked out.

That night, I learned the rest of the story. Word had spread that after I'd left, she'd gone back inside, red-faced and tearful, spinning a tale about how I'd held her down on the sidewalk and then abandoned her there. People rallied to her side. Nobody questioned her version.

And just like that, I was branded the offender.

The place I'd considered my weekend refuge became off-limits. Friends stopped texting when they went out there. Some even looked at me differently, as if the accusation itself was enough to stain me.

All because I'd said no. All because I hadn't let her have her way.

And the truth — the simple, ugly truth — was that nobody wanted to hear my side.

4. Store Girl

I was twenty years old, still figuring out how to be an "adult," when I landed a job as an assistant manager at a retail store in Salt Lake City. The place wasn't glamorous — neon lighting that buzzed faintly, racks of discount clothes, the smell of detergent mixed with stale air freshener — but it was steady work, and it paid my rent.

That's where I met her.

She was sixteen, one of the top sales associates. Everyone loved her. Customers asked for her by name.

My boss praised her nonstop, always pointing to her numbers as proof of her talent. And I'll admit, she was sharp — she could talk anyone into buying something they didn't need. But beneath that bubbly exterior, there was something else.

Something only I seemed to notice.

The first time it happened, I brushed it off. I was restocking a shelf when I felt a flick across my back — light, but unmistakable. Fingernails dragging over my shirt. I turned quickly, thinking someone had bumped me. There she was, smiling, eyes bright.

"Oops," she said, voice lilting, like it was just a joke.

I didn't laugh.

But it kept happening.

Whenever we worked the same shift, she was glued to me. If I walked to the backroom, she followed. If I went to check the registers, she trailed behind. If I crouched down to fix a display, I'd feel the scratch of her nails across my shoulders or lower back, as if she couldn't resist reminding me she was there.

"Cut it out," I'd say, keeping my voice low so no one else would hear.

She'd tilt her head, grin wider. "You don't like it?"

I did everything I could to avoid her — assigned her different tasks, made excuses to stay on the opposite end of the store. But somehow, she always found a way back to me.

I went to my superior.

"Listen," I said one afternoon in the cramped office, "we've got a problem. She won't leave me alone. She keeps touching me. Following me."

My boss didn't even look up from the report she was reading. "She's sixteen. She's just being friendly."

"It's not friendly," I pressed. "It's —"

"She's our top seller," my boss interrupted, finally meeting my eyes.

"She's valuable. Don't make this into something it's not."

The words stung. I was twenty, technically an adult, technically in charge when the manager wasn't around — but in that moment, I felt powerless.

So I kept my mouth shut.

Weeks went by. The behavior escalated. She grew bolder, reaching for my arms, brushing my sides when she walked past. Once, she grabbed my wrist and pressed my hand against her hip. I yanked it away like I'd touched a hot stove.

Nobody noticed. Or maybe nobody cared.

The breaking point came on a late shift. We were closing together — just the two of us. The store was quiet, the fluorescent lights buzzing overhead as we  counted tills and locked up registers.

I was in the backroom, sorting paperwork, when I felt her behind me. Too close. Her hand slid along my side, down my stomach, hovering lower.

My body went rigid.

"Stop," I barked, louder than I intended.

She laughed. Actually laughed. "You're so uptight. Don't you want to have a little fun?"

Her hand darted lower, aiming straight for me.

I stepped back sharply, hitting the shelf behind me. My heart was pounding in my ears. "Enough!"

And then, like some divine stroke of timing, the office door opened.

It was my boss. She had come by to check on closing.

Her eyes landed on us, and for the first time, she saw what I'd been trying to explain all along — the girl, hand extended toward me, frozen in guilty shock.

The silence lasted only a second, but it felt like an eternity.

"Out," my boss said, voice low and furious. "Now."

The girl's smile faltered. "But — "

"Now."

She left in a storm of muttered protests, her footsteps echoing down the hallway.

My boss turned to me. For once, there was no doubt in her face. No dismissal. No disbelief. Just a grim understanding.

"She's fired," she said.

I exhaled, the breath shaking out of me like I'd been holding it for weeks. Relief washed over me — but it was tangled with something else. Bitterness. Because it had taken that moment for anyone to believe me.

Not my words. Not my warnings. Only the sight of her hand, finally crossing the line in front of someone else.

She was gone the next day. Her sales record, her popularity — it didn't matter anymore. She'd vanished from the store like she'd never existed.

And yet, the unease lingered.

Whenever I walked through the aisles, I half-expected to feel nails tracing my back again. Whenever I worked a late shift, I glanced over my shoulder, waiting.

It was over. But it never really left me.

5. Party Girl

I was twenty-eight when one of my closest female friends decided to rent an apartment for her birthday party. She wanted a change from the usual bars and clubs — something more private, something that felt like hers. By the time I finished a late shift at work and drove over, the party was already in full swing.

The apartment buzzed with noise: music thumping from a Bluetooth speaker, people laughing too loudly in the kitchen, glasses clinking as bottles of cheap liquor were passed around. I shrugged off my jacket and stepped inside, expecting the usual cozy chaos of old friends celebrating.

Instead, my eyes landed on her.

A girl I didn't recognize — slumped on the couch, drink in hand, hair wild, eyes unfocused. She looked wrecked. Wasted beyond the point of fun, teetering in that messy space where every movement seemed both sloppy and deliberate.

But what caught my attention wasn't her condition. It was the way everyone else behaved around her.

My guy friends — normally loud, relaxed, quick with jokes — stood stiff and awkward against the far wall, as if keeping as much distance from her as possible.

I drifted over. "Okay, what's going on here? Who is she?"

They exchanged looks, grimaces. One of them muttered, "Red flag. Stay clear."

"Why?" I pressed.

Another leaned closer. "She keeps grabbing people. Hands

everywhere. Butts, crotches — you name it." He shuddered. "Won't leave anyone alone."

I glanced back at the girl. She was laughing at nothing, tossing her hair back, spilling half her drink down her shirt. She looked like a caricature of "the drunk party guest," but there was an edge to it — something invasive in the way her eyes tracked people moving around her.

Meanwhile, the birthday girl, my friend, was already several shots deep herself. She didn't notice the problem. She was busy clinking glasses, hugging friends, swaying to the music.

So the rest of us ignored the stranger. More friends arrived, filling the space with chatter and energy, and for a while the mood lifted. The unwanted guest sat in the corner like a storm cloud, but nobody engaged.

Until she made her move on me.

I was standing near the kitchen counter, sipping my drink, when I felt a sudden grip from behind. Firm. Unmistakable.

I froze, every muscle locking up.

Her hand was on me.

I spun around to find her grinning, eyes glazed but mischievous. She didn't say a word. She didn't need to. The look on her face said it all — like I was just another target in her drunk game.

"Don't touch me," I snapped, louder than I meant.

She giggled. Actually giggled. And then, as if on cue, she moved on to the next guy who walked past, lunging for him too.

It became a sick routine. Every man who came near was grabbed, pawed at, treated like her personal amusement park ride. Some shoved her away. Others just moved to the opposite end of the room, faces twisted with disgust.

But nobody wanted to be the one to make a scene. The tension built. Conversations faltered. The fun of the party thinned out, replaced by that unspoken why is this still happening? feeling.

Finally, fed up, we corralled the birthday girl.

"Hey," I said, pulling her aside. "You need to deal with her."

She blinked at me, tipsy and confused. "Her who?"

"The stranger who's been groping everyone all night!" one of my buddies added.

Our friend frowned, genuinely baffled. "Wait. Who is she?"

"You invited her, right?"

She shook her head. "I have no idea who that is, and honestly, I don't even know."

The realization hit all of us at once. This wasted girl — this menace who had ruined half the party's vibe — wasn't even on the guest list.

The birthday girl's expression hardened. Outrage cut through the alcohol fog. She marched straight over, planted herself in front of the intruder, and barked, "Out. Now. You're not welcome here."

The girl tried to protest, slurring excuses, but there was no saving her. She was ushered to the door, stumbling and whining as she went.

And just like that, the party breathed again.

Laughter returned. Music felt lighter. Drinks tasted better. The storm cloud had been thrown out, and the apartment reclaimed its joy.

But for me, the moment lingered. The memory of that hand grabbing me without consent, the brazen way she had treated every guy like an object — it stuck.

Not every red flag is obvious at first glance. But when every man in the room is already standing as far away as possible? Believe them.

6. Lonely Girl

Back in college, there was this girl who started sitting with me between classes. At first, it seemed harmless. We were both killing time before lectures, both hanging out in the same hallway with vending machines humming and students drifting past.

She was easy to talk to. We covered all the usual topics—classes, professors, the lousy cafeteria food. She'd ask about my schedule, I'd ask about hers. Nothing heavy. Nothing flirty. Just a couple of students passing time.

She wore a ring on her finger, though, and early on she mentioned her fiancé. She also had a baby, which surprised me. She was juggling coursework, a fiancé, and motherhood, all while showing up to class like it was nothing. I respected that.

That's why it threw me when she started inviting me to hang out.

"You should come over sometime," she said one afternoon, twirling a pen between her fingers.

"I've got work," I replied, brushing it off.

Another day: "You should meet my baby. She's so cute. You'd love her."

I laughed awkwardly. "I'm swamped. Maybe another time."

Truth was, I didn't want to meet her baby. I didn't want to get tangled up in her personal life. I wasn't interested, and I thought my polite refusals made that clear.

But she didn't stop.

The more we talked, the more personal she got. One week she told me about her fiancé—how he worked long hours, how he didn't "understand her." Another week, she complained about her parents and how they judged her for being engaged so young.

I mostly just listened. Nodded. Offered vague, neutral responses. The kind you give when you don't want to encourage someone but also don't want to be rude.

Still, she kept showing up, always sliding into the empty seat next to me, always waiting to catch me after class.

"You're a good listener," she said once, her eyes lingering on me in a way that made me uncomfortable.

I shrugged it off. "I just don't talk much."

But inside, I felt uneasy.

Then came the messages.

It started simple enough. Hey, what's up? Did you finish the reading? I'd reply briefly, usually one-word answers. I didn't want to fuel it, but ignoring her completely felt unnecessarily harsh.

One night, though, her tone shifted.

I think about you a lot, she wrote.

I frowned at the screen. My thumbs hovered over the keyboard, unsure how to respond.

Before I could figure it out, another message arrived: I don't want to be with him anymore. I want you.

My stomach dropped hard, like I'd swallowed a stone, my pulse racing as though I'd been cornered by something I never agreed to face.

This wasn't friendly. This wasn't casual. This was something else entirely, blurring into delusion I wanted no part of.

I typed back carefully: You're engaged. You've got a baby. I'm not interested.

She didn't stop.

You don't understand. He doesn't make me feel the way you do. You actually listen. You care.

I stared at those words, frustration building. I didn't care. Not like that. I'd been polite, reserved, civil, nothing more.

I tried again: I think you're confused. I've never flirted with you. I don't want anything like that.

Her reply came fast. Don't lie. I can tell you feel it too.

My jaw tightened. I didn't. Not even close. It felt like talking to a wall — her fantasy had no cracks.

The next day on campus, she cornered me outside the lecture hall.

"Did you get my messages?" she asked, voice bright but eyes searching.

"Yeah," I said carefully.

"So?"

"So... no. I don't feel that way. You have a family."

Her expression flickered. "You're just scared. You'd rather hide behind excuses."

"It's not an excuse," I snapped. "I don't want this."

She looked hurt for half a second, then her face hardened. "You will."

And with that, she walked off.

That night, my phone buzzed again.

Send me pics. You know... of your thing. Please.

I almost dropped the phone.

No.

Why not? Just one. I think about it all the time. I can't stop.

I clenched my teeth, typing: Stop messaging me.

But she didn't. The texts kept coming in waves. I want you. I need you. Please. Don't pretend you don't want me too.

My pulse quickened. Anger mixed with a strange, sour guilt, even though I knew I hadn't done anything wrong. But I felt trapped, like she'd somehow flipped the script and cast me as part of a story I'd never agreed to be in.

So I did the only thing I could think of.

I blocked her number. Blocked her online accounts. And the next morning, I dropped the class entirely.

I didn't explain to anyone. I didn't want to.

It felt like fleeing, but it also felt like the only way to reclaim peace of mind. If I kept showing up, she'd keep sitting next to me, keep waiting outside the lecture hall, keep messaging me from new numbers.

I couldn't risk it.

And the strangest part?

I never gave her any reason to think I wanted more. Not once. Not a joke, not a flirt, not a slip. I'd treated her like any other classmate.

But sometimes, loneliness twists people.

And I wasn't going to let her twist me into something I never signed up for.

7. Baby Girl

I was twenty years old, still figuring out life, and not exactly what you'd call "dating material." I had a  couple of steady routines — school, part-time work, the occasional night out with friends. I wasn't looking for anything serious, but I also wasn't opposed to meeting someone.

So when this woman — someone I barely knew, but who seemed

genuinely lovely in our brief chats — suggested we meet for dinner, I thought, Why not?

The restaurant wasn't fancy, just a mid-range place with booths and a decent menu, the kind of spot where first dates felt safe. I arrived right on time, sat down, and waited.

And waited.

Ten minutes passed. Fifteen. I pulled out my phone, scrolled aimlessly, checked the clock again. At the thirty-minute mark, I started to wonder if she'd stood me up. At forty-five, I considered leaving.

By the time an entire hour had passed, I'd already rehearsed what I'd say if she texted me later with some flimsy excuse. But then, finally, I saw her. She was weaving her way through the tables, purse over one arm — and on her other hip, balanced precariously, was a baby.

Her baby.

An eight-month-old, maybe. Round cheeks, drool-soaked bib, squirming restlessly as she shifted her weight to hold him.

I blinked. No warning. No mention. No "by the way." Just: Here's my kid, surprise.

She smiled as if nothing were out of the ordinary, slid into the booth across from me, and plopped the baby down beside her. "Sorry I'm late," she said breezily, adjusting her hair. "He was fussy."

I nodded dumbly, still catching up to reality.

The waitress came by and handed us menus. I tried to reorient myself, pretend this was normal. I asked about her day, her interests, her work. She gave short answers, sometimes just a shrug, while her baby banged a spoon against the table like it was a drum.

I kept talking — about classes, my job, hobbies — because the silence was unbearable. She just stared at me. Stared. Wide-eyed, locked in, like she was studying me under a microscope. I  don't think she blinked more than twice the entire time.

Meanwhile, her kid was staging a full-scale rebellion.

First it was whining. Then came the shrill cries, the flailing little fists, the red face. He threw his fork onto the floor, hurled his straw across the booth, then started grabbing at ice cubes from her glass and dropping them onto the table.

Other diners glanced over, brows furrowed.

I leaned back awkwardly, trying to finish my thought about work while dodging airborne projectiles.

What unsettled me most wasn't the tantrum — it was that she made no attempt to soothe him. No rocking, no shushing, no distraction with toys or snacks. She just sat there, chin propped in her hand, gazing at me like I was supposed to be performing.

The waitress came by, politely but firmly. "Ma'am, your baby's disturbing other guests. Could you maybe...?"

The girl just smiled, nodded faintly, and went right back to staring at me. The baby screamed louder.

I wanted to disappear under the table.

By the end of the meal, my nerves were shredded. I flagged the waitress for the check, and out of pure embarrassment — because I felt bad for her, bad for the staff, bad for the whole spectacle — I left a large tip.

We parted ways outside with a brief, awkward goodbye. I went home thinking, Well, that was one of the strangest dates I've ever had, but at least it's over.

Except it wasn't.

Later that night, my phone buzzed.

Her: You're... average.

I stared at the screen. Average?

Me: What does that mean?

Her: You talk too much. You don't engage with my baby. You're not daddy material.

I felt heat rising in my face, though I was alone in my room.

Me: This was our first date. Why would you even bring your baby without saying anything?

Her: If you can't handle him, you can't handle me. Simple.

I set the phone down and rubbed my temples. My brain replayed the dinner in high-definition: the shrieking, the flying utensils, her unblinking stare. She'd said almost nothing all evening, but apparently she'd been taking notes — grading me, like some warped audition for fatherhood I never signed up for.

Me: I'm not interested. Please don't text me again.

And then, without waiting for her reply, I blocked her number.

It wasn't until the next morning, after I'd slept on it, that the whole thing really sank in.

I was twenty years old. Twenty. Barely keeping my own life stitched together. And here she was, expecting me to step into some instant-family audition — unannounced, uninvited.

I realized, too, that she hadn't come looking for a date. She'd come looking for a replacement. A stand-in. Someone to slot neatly into the life she already had planned.

And that wasn't going to be me..

www.ingramcontent.com/pod-product-compliance
Lightning Source LLC
Chambersburg PA
CBHW040259240726
48664CB00006B/1307